CW01064489

Original title:
Reinventing Relationships

Copyright © 2024 Swan Charm
All rights reserved.

Author: Liisi Lendorav
ISBN HARDBACK: 978-9916-89-007-3
ISBN PAPERBACK: 978-9916-89-008-0
ISBN EBOOK: 978-9916-89-009-7

Resilient Embrace

In shadows deep, we find our light,
With open hearts, we hold on tight.
Through storms we bend, but never break,
Together we're strong, for love's own sake.

Every bruise becomes a crown,
In the trials, we won't back down.
With every fall, we rise anew,
An unyielding bond, just me and you.

The Art of Redefining Us

In echoes of what used to be,
We seek the truth, we set it free.
With every step, we carve a path,
Transforming pain into our math.

Old definitions fade away,
As we create a brand new way.
In the canvas of our dreams,
We paint with vibrant, hopeful beams.

Navigating New Currents

Across the waves of change we glide,
With trust and hope forever tied.
Through currents fierce, we find our course,
Our hearts united, a steady force.

Every twist brings strength anew,
In uncharted waters, we push through.
With sails unfurled, we brave the tides,
Together, love is where it resides.

Whispers of Renewal

In silence, whispers softly call,
Of fresh beginnings, we stand tall.
From ashes rise, a fragrant bloom,
In each new dawn, we banish gloom.

Nature's song, a soothing balm,
In this embrace, we find our calm.
With every breath, we start again,
In autumn's hush, we learn to mend.

Heartstrings Reshaped

In shadows deep, we find our light,
Echoes of dreams that take their flight.
Frayed edges mend, with gentle hands,
New melodies born, as hope expands.

Tender whispers, time’s soft embrace,
Heal the wounds, restore the grace.
Each strum a journey, each note a tear,
Heartstrings reshaped, banish the fear.

Harmonies of Hope

In the quiet dawn, the world awakes,
Promises bloom, where the heart breaks.
Voices unite in a fragrant song,
Together in strength, we carry along.

Each note a beacon, shining bright,
Guiding us through the longest night.
In every moment, love’s hand we hold,
Harmonies of hope, a story retold.

Crafting the Unexpected

From lines of chaos, beauty flows,
In the unknown, the heart bestows.
Whims of fate, with colors diverse,
Crafting the unexpected, life’s sweet verse.

Embrace the flaws, let laughter reign,
In every stumble, there’s joy in pain.
Pieces align, like stars in a night,
Creating a canvas, vivid and bright.

Awakened Reflections

In mirrored depths, the soul expands,
Discovering truths in foreign lands.
Layers peel back, revealing the core,
Awakened reflections, seeking for more.

Each gaze a journey, a tale to unfold,
Wisdom of ages, both brave and bold.
In stillness found, we rise above,
Awakened reflections, a dance of love.

A Journey Reimagined

With every step, new sights unfold,
Whispers of stories yet to be told.
Winding paths and gentle streams,
Awaken the heart, ignite our dreams.

Beneath the stars, we carve our fate,
Each moment lived, never too late.
Mountains tall and valleys deep,
In the journey's arms, our hopes we keep.

In laughter shared and silence borne,
Together we rise, together we mourn.
Through twists and turns, we find our way,
In every sunset, there's promise of day.

Canvas of Companions

Brushstrokes vibrant, colors entwine,
On this canvas, our souls combine.
Moments captured in hues so bright,
Together we paint our own starry night.

Shapes of laughter, shadows of tears,
A masterpiece formed through all our years.
Every glance, a stroke of fate,
Woven connections, bonds we create.

With every line, our stories blend,
In this art, there is no end.
Canvas of life, rich and diverse,
A celebration of who we are, not the worst.

Paths Less Traveled

Through tangled woods and unseen trails,
We wander onward, hearts with sails.
What lies ahead is yet unknown,
In paths less traveled, courage has grown.

With every choice, a lesson learned,
The flame of adventure, brightly burned.
Whispers of dreams in the twilight glow,
In the dance of risk, our spirits flow.

We forge our way, with faith as our guide,
In the quiet spaces, hope won't hide.
For in every stumble, a joy to find,
Paths less traveled, where souls unwind.

The Fabric of Understanding

Threads of kindness, woven tight,
In the loom of life, we find our light.
Patterns of love, intricate and strong,
In every heart, we all belong.

Through the tapestry, stories share,
Each unique strand, a bond so rare.
In patience held and compassion shown,
The fabric of understanding has grown.

When colors clash and voices rise,
We weave anew under open skies.
For in the threads of empathy spun,
Lies the hope of many, united as one.

Transformative Ties

In shadows cast by doubt's embrace,
We reach for light, for change, for grace.
With every thread, our stories weave,
Transforming fears, we dare believe.

In whispered hopes, our passions sing,
From fragile seeds, new dreams take wing.
Together strong, we break the mold,
Our journey bright with hearts of gold.

In moments shared, we build a bridge,
Across the gaps, we dare to ridge.
With open minds, our spirits soar,
Transformative ties forevermore.

The Symphony of Us

In harmony, we find our way,
A dance of souls, in bright array.
Each note we play, a story told,
Together bold, our hearts unfold.

Through highs and lows, our rhythms blend,
In perfect mix, our spirits mend.
A melody of trust and grace,
The symphony, our shared embrace.

As laughter echoes, tears subside,
With every heartbeat, love's our guide.
In every verse, our lives entwine,
The symphony of us, divine.

Reimagining Together

With distant dreams, we break the norm,
In tandem steps, we weather storm.
Imagination fuels our flight,
Reimagining the dark to light.

Each idea sparked, a flame ignites,
New paths to tread, new future sights.
United vision, hand in hand,
Together we will take a stand.

With open hearts, we paint anew,
A canvas bright, a vibrant hue.
In unity, we redefine,
Reimagining; hopes align.

Fresh Canvas, New Colors

On fresh canvas, our dreams unfold,
With colors bright, both brave and bold.
Each stroke a choice, a moment's grace,
New stories sprout in this vast space.

A splash of joy, a hint of blue,
Each brush of life, a dream come true.
Creating wonders with each draw,
In inspiration, we find awe.

With every layer, depth reveals,
The beauty born from how it feels.
Together we explore the flow,
Fresh canvas, new colors to show.

The Portrait of Us

In the frame of moments we stand,
Captured smiles in gentle light,
Brush strokes of laughter and time,
A canvas of love in our sight.

Each color tells a sweet tale,
Whispers of dreams wrapped in grace,
Together we paint a vivid path,
In the portrait of our embrace.

Seasons change but we remain,
The essence of us intertwined,
Through storms and sun, we endure,
A masterpiece uniquely designed.

With every glance, a memory glows,
The beauty in our shared days,
Our story written in hues,
In this gallery, forever stays.

As years pass, we'll still stand here,
In the frame, hand in hand,
The portrait of us will unfold,
An eternal love, perfectly planned.

Tapestry of Change

Threads of time weave through our lives,
Colors shift with every breath,
Patterns form from joys and strife,
In the tapestry, we find depth.

Each knot a story, every twist,
Embracing moments, both light and dark,
Together we craft what must exist,
A vibrant path, a lasting mark.

When shadows loom, we stitch with hope,
Creating beauty from what we fear,
In the fabric of now, we learn to cope,
With every challenge, we draw near.

Change dances through our woven hearts,
A rhythm found in life's parade,
As seasons fade and new ones start,
In this tapestry, dreams aren't swayed.

Through trials faced and laughter shared,
A rich design begins to show,
In the tapestry of change, we're dared,
To grow, evolve, and freely glow.

Unfolding Stories

Pages turn in whispered words,
Ink flows with a gentle grace,
Every chapter holds a spark,
Unfolding stories find their place.

Lines of joy and threads of pain,
Interwoven with hopes and fears,
Each paragraph holds a refrain,
Of lessons learned throughout the years.

In shadows cast and sunlight bright,
The plot thickens with every choice,
Characters dance in shared delight,
In every silence, we find voice.

With every story, a new dawn breaks,
Unraveling secrets, wide and deep,
The heart of life, each heartbeat wakes,
As we uncover what we keep.

A narrative of dreams and schemes,
In every moment, we have grown,
Unfolding tales become our beams,
In the book of us, we’re never alone.

Exploring Fresh Dimensions

Beyond horizons, new paths wait,
With every step, we forge ahead,
Curiosity fuels our hearts,
In fresh dimensions, we are led.

Infinity beckons with open arms,
New landscapes dance like stars at night,
In every corner, hidden charms,
We chase the glow, embrace the light.

Adventures call us to explore,
Uncharted lands, both wide and vast,
With open minds, we seek for more,
In the future's grasp, we are cast.

Through valleys deep and peaks so high,
We learn to soar, to bend, to break,
In every challenge, we learn to fly,
Each dimension embraced, no mistake.

Together wandering, hand in hand,
In unity, we dare to dream,
Exploring fresh dimensions grand,
In this journey, we find our theme.

Nurtured Bonds

In shadows cast by gentle light,
Two souls entwined, hearts take flight.
Through whispered words and soft embrace,
We find our home, a sacred space.

With every laugh, a memory blooms,
Together we face the loudest booms.
In silence shared, our joys ignite,
Nurtured bonds feel so right.

The Rebirth of Us

In fading echoes, memories sigh,
Underneath the vast, open sky.
With every heartbeat, a chance to renew,
The spark that once drew me to you.

Through trials faced and tears we've shed,
A garden of love now gently spread.
From ashes rose, our spirits soar,
The rebirth of us, forever more.

Awakening Affection

Amidst the dawn, soft hues of gold,
Awakening tales of love untold.
With every glance, the warmth we feel,
A silent promise, so deeply real.

In tender moments, our souls align,
Two hearts in rhythm, pure and divine.
Through every touch, affection grows,
In quiet depths, our passion flows.

Woven Whispers

In threads of time, our stories weave,
With whispered dreams, we dare believe.
Every secret, a tapestry bright,
Woven whispers embrace the night.

Through laughter shared and sorrows borne,
In each new dawn, our love reborn.
With every heartbeat, we softly bind,
Woven whispers, forever entwined.

New Beginnings

A dawn breaks soft and bright,
Whispers of the past take flight.
With each step, a choice to make,
A path anew, the fears will shake.

Seeds of hope in fertile ground,
Dreams arise without a sound.
Fresh horizons call us near,
A brighter life begins right here.

The air is crisp; the sky is clear,
With open hearts, we'll persevere.
Let go of what no longer serves,
Embrace the love that life deserves.

Together we will forge ahead,
New stories waiting to be said.
Every heartbeat, every breath,
A dance of life that conquers death.

New beginnings, fresh and bright,
With courage, we embrace the light.
Each moment is a brand new chance,
To live, to love, to dream, to dance.

Unspoken Threads

In silence, words can weave a bond,
A tapestry where hearts respond.
Invisible ties that hold us close,
In quiet moments, love engrossed.

The subtle glance, the knowing smile,
A language shared across each mile.
Though spoken words may drift away,
These threads we share will always stay.

A lingering touch, a gentle sigh,
Unvoiced feelings that can’t deny.
In shadows cast by fading light,
Our hearts connect, the power ignites.

Through trials faced and battles fought,
The strength of us needs not be taught.
In bonds we didn’t choose, we find,
Unspoken threads that intertwine.

When storms arise and paths grow dim,
These silent ties will never thin.
A fabric rich, in colors blend,
A story of love that has no end.

The Mosaic of Us

Each piece distinct, yet fit so right,
Together we create the light.
Fragments scattered, bold and bright,
A masterpiece beyond our sight.

In moments shared, our colors shine,
A blend of hearts, a sacred line.
From laughter's joy to sorrow's ache,
Our mosaic grows with every break.

Diverse in dreams and hopes we chase,
Unified in this sacred space.
Every story, every scar,
A stepping stone to who we are.

The world outside may fade away,
Within our hearts, we wish to stay.
As life unfolds, we stand not alone,
In every shard, our love has grown.

Together we'll embrace the vast,
The future bright, as shadows pass.
In every piece, a part of trust,
This painted life, the mosaic of us.

Echoes of Change

Leaves rustle softly in the breeze,
Nature hums its sweet decrees.
With every shift, a voice repeats,
Life's cycle flows, as time competes.

From dawn's first light to twilight's glow,
Each echo whispers what we know.
Embrace the shift, surrender fears,
The heart will guide through all the years.

In every challenge, lessons learned,
In every scar, the fire burned.
The past may haunt, but we will rise,
With open hearts and open skies.

Though storms may rage and tempests roar,
We'll find the strength to heal and soar.
In every ending, a chance to start,
Echoes remind us, trust your heart.

Change dances like the moon's soft glow,
In every ebb, there's space to grow.
So let us stir and let us sing,
In echoes sweet, the joy will spring.

The Canvas of Togetherness

Colors blend and swirl in light,
Each stroke whispers our shared flight.
Textures woven through the day,
In unity, we find our way.

Hands held tight, hearts collide,
In every hue, emotions ride.
With every shade, a story told,
In togetherness, we are bold.

Laughter painted on the wall,
In every session, we stand tall.
Brushes dance to a joyous beat,
Creating memories, bittersweet.

Every layer, every tone,
Crafts a tapestry we own.
In the gallery of our days,
Love's impression never decays.

Together we'll paint, side by side,
In harmony, our spirits glide.
The canvas echoes our embrace,
A masterpiece time cannot erase.

Pathways to Understanding

Winding roads beneath our feet,
Each step taken, a chance to meet.
Voices blend in whispered dreams,
In shadows, light softly beams.

Curiosity, our guiding star,
Leads us to places near and far.
Every difference a chance to share,
In this journey, we show we care.

Questions asked, and answers given,
In the maze of thoughts, we are driven.
Bridges built from heart to heart,
In understanding, we find our part.

With open minds, we explore new ground,
In every silence, there's a sound.
A tapestry of thoughts we weave,
In every bond, we must believe.

Each pathway leads us to the same,
In unity, we share our name.
With every step, we learn and grow,
In understanding, love will flow.

Fragments Reassembled

Scattered pieces, stories lost,
In the chaos, we count the cost.
With careful hands, we gather near,
Each fragment holds a trace of fear.

Shattered dreams, yet hope remains,
In every loss, resilience gains.
With patience, we stitch the seams,
Recreating our shattered dreams.

Through the cracks, the light will shine,
With every shard, a secret sign.
Together we'll reshape the past,
In unity, our shadows cast.

Finding beauty in the flawed,
In the silence, we are awed.
Through the fragments, we are whole,
In every piece, a story told.

With open hearts, we start anew,
In the mosaic, we see the true.
In fragments reassembled bright,
We find our strength, our guiding light.

Embracing the Unseen

In silence lies a world profound,
In quiet moments, truths are found.
Whispers of the heart take flight,
In shadows, dreams weave into light.

Beneath the surface, feelings dwell,
In hidden depths, we craft our spell.
Eyes may close, but spirits see,
In what's unseen, we find the key.

Unexpressed thoughts, a gentle breeze,
In every pause, a chance to tease.
With open arms, we dare to trust,
In the unseen, we rise from dust.

Every sigh, a story shared,
In the unvoiced, we are bared.
In the embrace of what we feel,
The unseen binds, the heart can heal.

Let us wander where shadows play,
In the unseen, we find our way.
With courage, we shall dive so deep,
In embracing all, our dreams we keep.

The Evolution of We

From whispers in the night,
To echoes loud and clear,
We crafted bonds in light,
Together, year by year.

We've woven dreams of hope,
In threads of shared delight,
With courage, we will cope,
And soar into the light.

Through trials, we have grown,
In unity, our strength,
A garden we have sown,
Together, at great length.

With every step we take,
A rhythm soft and true,
In love, we softly break,
And build the world anew.

So hand in hand, we stand,
In this grand tapestry,
Together, we have spanned,
The evolution of we.

Emerald Pathways

In the forest, green ablaze,
Emerald dreams take flight,
Where the sun, in golden rays,
Whispers secrets of the night.

Along the winding trails we roam,
Underneath the leafy veil,
Finding solace, finding home,
In the stories that unveil.

The breeze dances through the trees,
A symphony of peace,
Each step whispers gentle pleas,
In nature’s sweet release.

With every turn, a new delight,
A canvas rich and wide,
Emerald pathways shining bright,
Where heart and soul abide.

Together we shall wander far,
In this enchanted land,
Our spirits linked like a star,
In unity we stand.

Illuminating Connection

In the silence, sparks ignite,
A dance of souls unfolds,
With every word, a guiding light,
In vibrant hues, it molds.

Threads of laughter fill the air,
As hearts begin to blend,
In moments cherished, rare,
The warmth of love transcends.

Each glance tells a story sweet,
Of journeys intertwined,
In rhythm, our hearts repeat,
A bond that's undefined.

Through shadows, we will find our way,
Illuminated by trust,
In every dawn, a new display,
Together we adjust.

So let us weave this tapestry,
With threads both bold and fine,
In every stitch, a memory,
A love that will not decline.

Reframing Our Story

In the chapters we write, we find our way,
Old tales twisted into bright new days.
Each word a brush that colors the past,
Reframing our story, a spell that will last.

Through shadows that linger, we carve out the light,
Finding the courage to stand and to fight.
Embracing our scars, each lesson learned here,
Every heartbeat resounding, we shatter our fear.

Hope drapes around us like warm, tender seams,
Mending the fragments, we build our bright dreams.
With voices united, we soar in full flight,
Together we flourish, igniting the night.

In whispers of doubt, we echo our trust,
Building foundations of love, strong and just.
Reframing our story, a dance we will weave,
With every new chapter, we learn to believe.

With laughter and tears, we paint our own fate,
Every moment we share, we nurture and cultivate.
From dreams stitched together, we rise and we soar,
Reframing our story, forever, we explore.

Chameleon Love

In the heart's garden, colors blend and sway,
Chameleon love shifts with the light of the day.
A tender embrace that grows and then bends,
Adapting to seasons, that never quite ends.

In laughter, it sparkles, in tears, it runs deep,
A river of hues, where secrets we keep.
With every new sunrise, new shades we shall find,
Chameleon love, beautifully unconfined.

It thrives in the silence, it dances in sound,
A rhythm of whispers, where true joy is found.
In every transition, resilience will thrive,
In the heart of each moment, our spirits alive.

Like leaves in the autumn, we change as we grow,
Embracing transformation, both soft and aglow.
With every shade shuffled, our spirits entwine,
Chameleon love shines, endlessly divine.

Through storms and through rainbows, we journey as one,
In the tapestry woven, our colors are spun.
Chameleon love, forever we share,
In the art of connection, we find that we care.

Evolving Embraces

In the arms of change, we learn how to grow,
Evolving embraces, like rivers that flow.
With each gentle touch, we soften the night,
Respecting the journey, we bring forth the light.

Moments of silence carry weight that we share,
An unspoken bond wrapped in tender care.
As vines intertwine, our hearts beat as one,
In evolving embraces, two souls merge as sun.

With laughter and tears, we nurture and play,
In the fabric of time, we're finding our way.
New paths we uncover, horizons that gleam,
Evolving embraces, woven from dreams.

In letting the past shift, we gather the now,
Each lesson a thread, in unity we vow.
To cherish the journey, to honor it all,
With evolving embraces, we rise when we fall.

Together we flourish, hand in hand we stride,
In the tapestry of life, where love can't abide.
With open hearts facing what lies in our fate,
Evolving embraces, together we create.

The Palette of Togetherness

In the colors of love, we paint our own fate,
The palette of togetherness resonates.
With strokes of compassion, we blend and we share,
Creating a masterpiece, shaped by our care.

Sparks of connection, colors bright and bold,
Through laughter and stories, our truths are told.
Every hue a heart, every shade a soul's dream,
In the palette of togetherness, we flow like a stream.

From shadows to highlights, we balance the light,
In the art of our journey, we shine ever bright.
With warmth of our voices, we echo our song,
In the palette of togetherness, where we all belong.

With every brushstroke, new visions arise,
We color the world, see through each other's eyes.
Embracing the vibrant, the loud, and the meek,
The palette of togetherness whispers what we seek.

In unity crafted, our hearts intertwine,
Creating a canvas where love will define.
In the palette of dreams, the colors express,
Together we flourish, in love we invest.

Blossoms of Change

In gardens where new dreams ignite,
Soft petals dance in morning light.
Each color tells a story bold,
Of whispered hopes and tales of old.

The winds carry sweet scents near,
Awakening hearts, dispelling fear.
With every bloom, a fresh embrace,
Change unfolds at nature's pace.

Beneath the boughs of ancient trees,
Transformation rides on gentle breeze.
Roots intertwine in silent grace,
Life's cycles weave a vibrant space.

In shadows deep, where doubts reside,
New branches stretch, with arms open wide.
Claiming the sky, they reach and strive,
In every end, new beginnings thrive.

So let us tend our inner ground,
Nurture seeds of love profound.
For in our hearts, the promise springs,
Of blossoms bright and change that sings.

The Art of Becoming Us

Two souls meet in a gentle glow,
Crafting dreams in the ebb and flow.
With every laugh, a truth unfolds,
In the tapestry of stories told.

Shared moments, like threads entwined,
Colors blend, a masterpiece designed.
The art of us, a dance in time,
Composed in rhythm, a heartfelt rhyme.

When shadows fall, and silence drapes,
Through every challenge, love escapes.
Together we face, we break, we mend,
Two hearts as one, on each we depend.

As seasons change, so do we grow,
With every step, new depths to show.
An ever-evolving, boundless sea,
In every heartbeat, the art of we.

With every whisper, every sigh,
In this canvas, we learn to fly.
Hand in hand, through life we roam,
In the bond we build, we find our home.

Navigating New Waters

Set sail on seas of dreams unknown,
Each wave a chance for seeds to be sown.
With stars as our guide, and hearts so true,
Together we venture, just me and you.

In storms that rage, we'll find our way,
With courage as our light each day.
The horizon calls us, bold and bright,
A canvas waiting for daring flight.

Each swell and crest, a lesson learned,
Through trials faced, our spirits turned.
With sails unfurled and hopes set high,
We'll navigate through every sky.

In quiet coves, we'll drop anchor down,
Share secrets soft, without a frown.
Embracing the stillness, we'll reflect,
In the heart of the voyage, we connect.

As tides may change, so do we grow,
The map of life, our hearts will show.
With every journey, new paths to trace,
Navigating waters, we find our place.

Reweaving the Ties

Threads of friendship, pulled so tight,
In woven patterns, bathed in light.
Through laughter shared and tears we shed,
We stitch our tales, our hearts are fed.

In moments brief, connections spark,
A tapestry shines, though times are dark.
Through trials faced, our bond does grow,
Reweaving ties, our spirits flow.

With each embrace, we mend the seams,
In quiet nights, we share our dreams.
Together we rise, in harmony,
Crafting a legacy, bold and free.

In frayed edges, we find our strength,
Gathering courage, we'll go the length.
For every thread, a story spun,
In this rich weave, we are as one.

So let us cherish every thread,
Reweaving ties, where love is fed.
In every heartbeat, we find our ways,
Together we flourish, through all our days.

Echoing Futures

In the hush of night, dreams collide,
Soft whispers of hope, they won't hide.
Each echo a promise, each star a guide,
Together they dance, futures dignified.

Paths intertwine in the silent glow,
Choices alight, with seeds to sow.
Time's gentle hand, there's so much to know,
Through echoes of laughter, our spirits grow.

Moments like raindrops, falling unseen,
Painting our lives with colors so keen.
In every heartbeat, a world so serene,
Echoing futures, where love intervenes.

The dawn brings the light, a warm embrace,
Each step with purpose, finding our place.
In this vast expanse, let's quicken our pace,
For in these echoes, we find our grace.

Dreams stretching wide, like wings in the sky,
With every heartbeat, we learn how to fly.
In the arms of tomorrow, we reach and we try,
Echoing futures, where hopes never die.

Finding Harmony in Dissonance

In the clamor of life, notes clash and break,
Yet in the chaos, a rhythm can wake.
A symphony born from what seems a mistake,
Finding harmony where few would partake.

Voices aligned, each story unique,
In dissonant chords, true beauty can speak.
Together they weave, a tapestry sleek,
Finding our place in the spaces we seek.

Fractured and bold, the sound must endure,
With every embrace, there's strength to procure.
In hearts intertwined, we're learning for sure,
Finding harmony in the noise, we secure.

The contrast sings loud, but listen with care,
For in every discord, there's love to share.
Out of the shadows, a light we will flare,
Finding the balance, our souls laid bare.

Beneath all the chaos, a song will emerge,
A celebration of life, where differences merge.
Together we rise, on this vibrant surge,
Finding harmony, as dissonance purges.

Light Through Shadows

In quiet corners, shadows reside,
Yet glimmers of hope, in darkness, they bide.
A flicker of warmth, where dreams can abide,
Light through shadows, where fears once hide.

Each moment a chance, for courage to bloom,
Illuminating paths, dispelling the gloom.
A dance of the sun, through night's heavy loom,
Bringing forth petals, sweet scent of perfume.

In the tapestry dark, bright threads intertwine,
Weaving the stories of yours and of mine.
With light as our guide, we seek and we find,
Through shadows we travel, our hearts aligned.

The world whispers secrets, in sighs of the breeze,
A blend of the light, within rustling leaves.
In every heartbeat, a promise it weaves,
Light through shadows, where hope never leaves.

Embrace the light that will always remain,
Through storms and through silence, through joy and through pain.
In shadows we wander, but never in vain,
For light through the darkness will always sustain.

The Unfolding Journey

With every dawn, a blank page appears,
Written with laughter, sometimes with tears.
In the unfolding, we conquer our fears,
The journey invites us, our heart it steers.

Paths not yet taken, horizons abound,
In every step forward, new wonders are found.
With courage as compass, our spirits unbound,
The unfolding journey, where dreams resound.

Through valleys and peaks, the stories we share,
Moments of solitude, joined with a prayer.
In the dance of time, life's rhythm is rare,
Embracing each twist, with love laid bare.

The miles stretch ahead, yet we choose to roam,
In every new corner, we build a new home.
With hearts open wide, through the world we comb,
The unfolding journey, where we all belong.

Together we'll wander, with stars as our eyes,
In the tapestry woven, our hopes will arise.
With every adventure, the spirit defies,
The unfolding journey, a gift in disguise.

A Tale of Two Souls

In shadows deep, they found their way,
Two hearts that beat, come what may.
With whispered dreams, they shared their fears,
Together they laughed, and dried their tears.

Through twisting paths, their bond did grow,
In silent nights, the stars would glow.
Each promise made, a sacred vow,
Forever linked, they knew somehow.

In storms of life, they stood as one,
A dance of balance, they've just begun.
With hands entwined, they faced the night,
In love's embrace, they found their light.

Through valleys low, and mountains high,
With courage strong, they dared to fly.
Each moment shared, a treasure rare,
In every glance, a love laid bare.

As time flows on, their journey flows,
In every laugh, their spirit knows.
Together still, through thick and thin,
A tale of two souls, forever begins.

Altered Horizons

The sunrise breaks with colors bright,
A canvas new, igniting the night.
Beyond the hills, the world expands,
In whispered dreams, we make our plans.

With every step, the future calls,
Through open doors, our spirit sprawls.
We chase the dawn, the sky our friend,
On altered paths, we'll twist and bend.

With courage bold, we paint the skies,
In vibrant hues, our laughter flies.
As shadows fall, we hold the light,
In every heart, the hope ignites.

The road ahead, uncertain yet,
In moments lived, no room for regret.
With dreams to weave, and souls to bind,
In altered horizons, joy we find.

Let clouds roll in, let storms arise,
In fierce embrace, we find the ties.
For through the rain, our spirits soar,
Together still, we seek for more.

The Power of Connection

In every glance, a spark ignites,
Unseen threads weave through the nights.
With laughter shared, the world feels light,
In silent moments, souls take flight.

Through gentle words, our hearts align,
In whispered hopes, the stars entwine.
A touch, a smile, a bond so true,
In every pulse, I'm linked to you.

With open arms, we face the storm,
In unity found, we feel the warm.
For in each heartbeat, the truth we find,
The power of connection, forever blind.

As seasons change, our roots grow deep,
In shared embrace, our journey keeps.
Through joys and trials, we stand as one,
In every challenge, love has won.

So let us dance through life's embrace,
With every step, in this sacred place.
For in our hearts, a flame will glow,
The power of connection, in every flow.

Sails Adjusted

With winds of change, the sails are set,
We face the sea, no room for regret.
Through whispered tides, our course defined,
In dreams of gold, our hearts aligned.

The horizon calls, a siren's song,
With courage bold, we move along.
Each wave a rhythm, a dance of fate,
In every challenge, we navigate.

The stars above, our guiding light,
In boundless depths, the spark ignites.
We'll chart our course, through night and day,
With sails adjusted, we'll find our way.

Through stormy skies, we hold on tight,
In tempest's roar, we seek the light.
With laughter shared, and burdens eased,
In every heart, the journey's pleased.

As shores appear, our spirits rise,
With lessons learned, we claim the prize.
For every voyage, a tale to spin,
With sails adjusted, our lives begin.

Shifting Sands of Connection

In the desert of dreams, we stand,
Together on shifting, golden sand.
Waves of time wash over our feet,
Yet in the stillness, our hearts meet.

Veils of mirage drift in the air,
Drawing us closer, revealing our care.
With every grain, a story unfolds,
In whispers of warmth, each secret enfolds.

Beneath the sun's relentless gaze,
Our laughter dances in a gentle haze.
Through the currents, we navigate fate,
Binding our souls, we celebrate.

As shadows lengthen and dusk descends,
The horizon sings of us as friends.
In connection deeper than words could weave,
Together, forever, we choose to believe.

So let the winds shift, let them roam,
In our hearts, we've found our home.
The sands may change, but love withstands,
Eternal, in shifting sands, our hands.

Hearts in Bloom

In a garden where whispers play,
Hearts unfurl in a vibrant display.
Petals soft under the morning light,
In colorful silence, they take flight.

Each bloom tells a tale of its own,
In the language of love, seeds are sown.
From tender roots, connections grow,
Nurtured by kindness, they tend to glow.

The laughter of petals dances in air,
Every moment cherished, each breath a prayer.
In the garden of friendship, time slows down,
With hearts entwined in nature's crown.

As seasons shift, yet still we stand,
Together through life's shifting sand.
In every bud, a promise true,
We blossom anew, just me and you.

With every sunrise, joy starts to loom,
In the embrace of love, our hearts in bloom.
Forever nestled in sunlight's embrace,
Together we flourish in sweet, sacred space.

Uncharted Bonds

In the wilds of life, we roam afar,
Mapping the paths beneath a single star.
With each step taken on trails unknown,
The seeds of trust and friendship are sown.

Through winding roads and hidden creeks,
In every silence, it's connection that speaks.
Hearts untethered find strength to soar,
Discovering together what life has in store.

In the brush of the trees, in the mountains high,
We explore uncharted lands, just you and I.
With dreams as our compass, we journey wide,
Creating a bond that won't be denied.

Though storms may gather, and shadows fall,
In the face of uncertainty, our spirits stand tall.
Hand in hand, we conquer the unknown,
With courage and love, our true selves are shown.

In the tapestry woven, our threads intertwine,
Uncharted bonds form, yours and mine.
In every adventure, we ignite our flame,
Together we rise, unafraid of the same.

Threads of Transformation

In the loom of time, each stitch is fate,
Threads of life weave our stories innate.
Changing colors with every breath,
Transforming beauty through life and death.

Faded memories blend with the new,
A tapestry rich in each hue.
Every hardship a delicate thread,
Binding our journeys, where we tread.

With scissors poised, we cut away fears,
Embracing the shift, through laughter and tears.
In the patterns of growth, we find our place,
Woven together in love's embrace.

As fabrics shift, and seasons mold,
Stories of courage in threads of gold.
Transformations echo in every seam,
In the heart of the quilt, we stitch our dream.

So let the threads twist, let them turn,
In the fire of change, brightly we burn.
Through each transformation, we are reborn,
Threads of our lives, in unity, worn.

Navigating Change

Waves of time crash and roll,
Shifting sands within my soul.
Footprints fade as seasons blend,
Learning to embrace the bend.

New horizons lie ahead,
Paths once traveled, now misread.
Courage blooms among the fears,
Strengthened roots through all the years.

The map of life is drawn anew,
Each turn whispers, 'Find what's true.'
Guided by the stars above,
Carried forth by hope and love.

Pieces of me scatter wide,
Yet in change, I will confide.
With open arms, I greet the flow,
A heart that dares to rise and grow.

Through the storms and silent nights,
Emerging from the dark delights.
Navigating with a steady hand,
Finding joy in shifting sand.

Without a Map

Lost in the wild, the path unclear,
Wanderers chase the dreams held dear.
Each step forward, a leap of faith,
Trusting the heart, charting a wraith.

The compass spins, the stars may hide,
Yet whispers of hope will be my guide.
Every twist is a chance to learn,
In the unknown, the passions burn.

Every choice, both faint and bold,
Stories unfold, a journey told.
With every stumble, wisdom gained,
In trials, resilience is claimed.

Rivers cross and mountains rise,
Each detour brings new surprise.
Eyes wide open to what may come,
In this adventure, I find my home.

What lies ahead is yet unseen,
Embracing the chaos, I breathe in between.
A traveler's heart, with dreams untold,
Finding magic in the unrolled.

Fostering Growth

From tiny seeds, great wonders spring,
With gentle hands, I tend and sing.
Sunlight dances on fertile ground,
In nurturing love, strong roots are found.

Patience drapes the budding leaves,
In time, the heart learns how to breathe.
Every droplet of care will thrive,
In the embrace of life, we strive.

The rains may fall and winds may gust,
Yet in this soil, I place my trust.
Through trials, resilience will grow,
Beauty in the struggle will show.

Together we rise, both hand in hand,
In a garden where dreams take stand.
With each bloom, a story unfolds,
A tale of life, in colors bold.

Fostering dreams, we chart our fate,
In seasons of change, we celebrate.
Every moment a chance to find,
The strength in unity, intertwined.

Untangling Emotions

Threads of feelings, tightly sewn,
In the depths where sorrows groan.
Waves of joy and tides of pain,
In this tapestry, all remain.

Through the knots, my heart will weave,
Learning to let go, to believe.
Each color bright, each shadowed hue,
A reflection of the soul that's true.

Voices whisper, shadows play,
Untangling what I've kept at bay.
In vulnerable moments, I find the light,
Navigating through the darkest night.

With every tear, a thread is pulled,
Releasing chains, the heart is schooled.
In the chaos, harmony thrives,
Emotions dance, reminding lives.

Now I gather the twisted strands,
Crafting peace with open hands.
Embracing all, in joy and strife,
Untangling emotions, a tapestry of life.

Rediscovering Us

In the quiet nights we share,
Memories dance in the air.
Laughter echoes through the dark,
Flickers bright with every spark.

Time has woven our story fine,
Each stitch a moment, each thread a line.
Hand in hand, we walk the way,
Rediscovering love, day by day.

Whispers soft beneath the moon,
Hearts aligned, a sweet tune.
Past shadows fade in dawn's embrace,
Together we find our sacred space.

Through trials faced and mountains climbed,
In the rhythm of love, we're perfectly timed.
With every heartbeat, a brand new start,
Rediscovering us, soul to heart.

The place where all is known,
A garden of love, deeply sown.
We'll nurture this bond, watch it grow,
In the light of our own sweet glow.

The Alchemy of Affection

In the crucible of everyday,
We forge our love, come what may.
With every glance, a secret shared,
Transforming moments, love declared.

In laughter's warmth, joy ignites,
Turning shadows into lights.
Each tender kiss, a potion rare,
Mixing dreams in the evening air.

The alchemy of hearts so true,
Turns mundane into something new.
With every challenge, we will rise,
As golden threads weave through our lives.

In silence deep, our spirits blend,
A magic born, on love we depend.
Together, storms can't break our trust,
In this great alchemy, it's love or bust.

With every heartbeat, we unfold,
Stories of warmth in this world so cold.
Together we stand, forever as one,
In life's alchemical dance, we've just begun.

Building Bridges Anew

In the twilight, dreams take flight,
Hearts entwined, we chase the light.
With open arms, we span the space,
Building bridges, our sacred place.

Each whispered hope, a sturdy beam,
Crafting futures from every dream.
Brick by brick, we rise and soar,
With love as our guide, we find the door.

Through storms that came, we’ve weathered well,
In every challenge, our stories dwell.
With laughter shared and tears we’ve shed,
Building bridges, where fears have fled.

Hand in hand, we cross the divide,
In our hearts, this love we bide.
With every step, a promise made,
In unity, never afraid.

As sunsets cast upon our path,
We find strength in love's sweet math.
Through every trial, through every view,
Building bridges anew, me and you.

Shadows and Sunlight

In the dance of shadows, we find our place,
Light and dark twine, a gentle embrace.
In laughter's glow and sorrow's sigh,
We navigate moments as time slips by.

Through fleeting days of joy and pain,
Love remains, our sweetest gain.
In twilight whispers, secrets unfold,
Stories of warmth when the night grows cold.

Sunlight breaks through, a golden stream,
Illuminating hopes, igniting a dream.
For every shadow that stretches long,
With every heartbeat, we sing our song.

We dance in rhythms of loss and grace,
Finding solace in love's embrace.
With every step, we'll weave our tale,
Through shadows cast and light unveiled.

In this journey, both bright and stark,
We'll light the way through the dark.
Together we rise, hearts intertwined,
In the balance of shadows and sunlight, we find.

Finding Common Ground

In shadows cast by doubt, we stand,
Seeking voices, hand in hand.
Through whispers soft, we hear the call,
Together we'll rise, never fall.

The world is vast, yet hearts can find,
A bridge uniting, unconfined.
With every step, our paths align,
In harmony, we'll intertwine.

With open minds, we'll learn to see,
The beauty in diversity.
Each story shared, a thread we weave,
Creating trust that won't deceive.

Though echoes of the past may scream,
We dare to hope, we dare to dream.
In laughter, tears, our spirits bind,
A testament to humankind.

So let us gather, side by side,
Embrace the journey, take the ride.
For in this search, we come to know,
The strength in love as we let go.

Embracing the Unfamiliar

A world unknown, it calls to me,
With hidden treasures yet to see.
I take a breath, and step across,
To find a path, no fear, no loss.

Each shadow speaks of tales untold,
In the warmth of dusk, in the bold.
With open heart, I dare to roam,
In the strange, I find my home.

The colors blend, the scents entwine,
In every corner, something divine.
I greet the new, with arms held wide,
In the unexpected, I take pride.

Though comfort wraps like a gentle song,
I know that change is never wrong.
In all the chaos, joy can bloom,
From unfamiliarity, I assume.

So let me wander, let me explore,
Each step I take opens a door.
In the vast unknown, I choose to stay,
Embracing life in every way.

Space for Growth

In silence lies a chance to breathe,
Where dreams can sprout, where minds believe.
A garden nurtured with gentle care,
In every heart, a seed to share.

With roots that delve into the ground,
We learn to rise, our purpose found.
Each challenge faced, a lesson learned,
In every twist, the passion burned.

The space we carve can shape our fate,
In solitude, we contemplate.
With open hearts, we stretch and reach,
In every struggle, life will teach.

Embracing change, we learn to bend,
In every sunset, a chance to mend.
Through seasons turning, we will grow,
Beyond the limits, we'll bestow.

So plant the dreams within this space,
And watch them flourish at their pace.
Together we'll rise, together we'll seek,
In every shadow, light will speak.

Love's Renaissance

In whispers soft, a love awakes,
With gentle hands, the heart remakes.
Through trials faced and tempests tossed,
In every moment, never lost.

The flame ignites, a bright new dawn,
In tangled paths, we'll carry on.
Together strong, we'll face the night,
In love's embrace, we find our light.

With every heartbeat, time rewinds,
In every glance, a truth unwinds.
With courage bold, we'll weave our tale,
In every storm, our ship won't sail.

A tapestry of dreams and sighs,
In laughter shared, the spirit flies.
Through seasons changing, hand in hand,
In love's renaissance, we will stand.

So let us dance to passion's song,
In every note, where we belong.
Through depths unknown, our spirits soar,
In love's embrace, forevermore.

A New Dawn of Us

In the sky, the colors blend,
A horizon where dreams extend.
With each breath, we find our way,
Together, we'll embrace the day.

The stars that twinkle in the night,
Guide our hearts, ignite our light.
Hand in hand, we take our stand,
A journey mapped by love so grand.

Let the sun kiss the morning dew,
Whispers of hope in skies so blue.
With each step, we write our song,
In this place where we belong.

Through shadows cast, we rise anew,
With every challenge, we push through.
The path ahead, a canvas wide,
In the dawn of us, we confide.

With laughter shared, and tears we shed,
Our story blooms, no words unsaid.
In this new dawn, we'll find our way,
Forever bright, come what may.

Infinite Possibilities

Within the silence, dreams take flight,
A canvas born of pure delight.
Endless paths stretch far and wide,
With open hearts, we dare decide.

Every choice is a seed we sow,
In the garden of what we know.
Together we explore the vast,
In every moment, hold on fast.

What if the stars could guide our path?
What if we smile in aftermath?
With courage strong, we chase the gleam,
In a world where we dare to dream.

A spectrum bright, a rainbow's arc,
Creates the light that sparks the dark.
With each heartbeat, let hope arise,
In infinite skies, our dreams shall rise.

Step by step, we forge ahead,
In every whisper, possibilities spread.
With eyes wide open, we explore,
What lies beyond is worth fighting for.

Threads of Connection

In a world where souls entwine,
We weave our thoughts, gently align.
A tapestry of voices true,
Each thread a story made for two.

Through laughter shared, and sorrow's ache,
The bonds we form will never break.
With every heartbeat, pulses flow,
In this web of love, we grow.

Through distance felt, and time apart,
The threads remain within the heart.
A connection deep, a silent vow,
No matter where, here and now.

In quiet moments, we find our peace,
In every glance, our fears release.
Together, always, we stand strong,
In this song of life, we belong.

With hands held tight, we face the storm,
In unity, our hearts keep warm.
Through every trial, we shall persist,
In this dance of love, we coexist.

Pioneering Together

With eyes set forth on paths unknown,
We take the leap, our seeds are sown.
In courage found, we face the night,
Side by side, we find our light.

With every step, the world unfolds,
Stories waiting to be told.
In each moment, challenges rise,
But together, we claim the skies.

Through endless trials, we will grow,
A daring spirit in each flow.
Innovation leads where fear retreats,
In this journey, our bond completes.

With open hearts, we venture wide,
In unison, we cast aside.
Adventure calls, our spirits soar,
Pioneering dreams to explore.

Through thick and thin, we pave the way,
In this dance of life, come what may.
Together, we'll herald a new day,
In unity, we find our way.

A Canvas of Us

In the twilight glow, we paint our dreams,
Strokes of laughter blend in soft streams.
Colors of whispers fill the night air,
Each moment captured with tender care.

Beneath the stars, our stories unfold,
Threads of our love, in portraits bold.
Canvas of memories, vibrant and bright,
We create our world, bathed in light.

With each new dawn, the colors shift,
A masterpiece born of love's sweet gift.
Together we flourish, hand in hand,
On this canvas, we take our stand.

Seasons may change, but we remain,
Mixed in the hues of joy and pain.
An artwork eternal, yours and mine,
A canvas of us, forever divine.

Awakening Together

In the stillness of dawn, we find our way,
Awakening softly, to greet the day.
With gentle smiles, we share the sun,
Two hearts ignited, becoming one.

Whispers of dreams float on the breeze,
Carried by hope, with such ease.
In each other's eyes, reflections gleam,
Awakening together, lost in a dream.

Moments of silence, a sacred bond,
In this awakening, we are fond.
Every heartbeat sings a sweet refrain,
Together we rise, through joy and pain.

Hand in hand, we explore what’s near,
Each step a promise, banishing fear.
Awakening souls in the early light,
Together we soar, taking flight.

Uncharted Intimacies

In the depths of night, we chart our course,
Through uncharted waters, a steady force.
Connecting our hearts, we navigate the tide,
In the unknown, our souls collide.

Every secret shared, a treasure found,
In these uncharted worlds, we're tightly bound.
With laughter and tears, we chart the vast,
Creating a map from our shared past.

In the closeness found, we boldly explore,
Unraveling mysteries, wanting more.
With each soft glance, we redefine,
Uncharted intimacies, yours and mine.

Through tangles of doubt, we make our way,
Building a bridge where shadows play.
In this adventure, our spirits soar,
Discovering depths, forever in awe.

The Dance of Change

In the rhythm of time, we sway and spin,
Embracing the new, letting go of the thin.
Footsteps align, as seasons unfold,
The dance of change, a story retold.

With every twist, we learn to adapt,
Finding our balance, within the unwrapped.
In harmony's pulse, we find our way,
The dance of change, leading each day.

Moments may falter, but we continue on,
With each beat of hope, a new dawn.
Through wild tempests, we learn to sway,
The dance of change, brightening the gray.

Together we move, close and apart,
Every step taken, a piece of our heart.
In this grand ballet, we will engage,
With grace, we embrace the dance of change.

A New Chapter Unwritten

Blank pages await, quiet and still,
Dreams dance gently, waiting to spill.
With each stroke of pen, a voice will rise,
In hues of hope, beneath open skies.

Moments unfolding, stories to weave,
In laughter and tears, we learn to believe.
Paths yet to travel, sides yet to see,
With each step forward, we become free.

Echoes of whispers, guiding our way,
In shadows of doubt, we cherish the day.
Together we journey, hearts intertwined,
In this grand adventure, new worlds we find.

Each chapter we write, a tale of our own,
In the fabric of time, our essence is sewn.
With courage ignited, we'll break through the grim,
For in each new beginning, the chances are slim.

So let us embrace, the unwritten page,
Where stories unfold, in every age.
Trust in the journey, and let go of fear,
A new chapter waits, and it starts right here.

Boundless Connections

Strings of affection, woven with care,
Across every distance, a bond we share.
Hearts like constellations, lighting the night,
In the vastness of life, you are my light.

Through laughter and sorrow, we stand hand in hand,
In the rhythm of moments, together we've planned.
With whispers of hope, we chase down our dreams,
In the dance of existence, nothing's as it seems.

Emotions like rivers, flow strong and true,
Carving through valleys, creating anew.
With every connection, a tapestry spun,
Uniting our stories, two souls become one.

Through bridges of trust, we boldly explore,
The depths of the heart, its infinite core.
In kindness and laughter, we find our way home,
Together forever, no need to roam.

A circle of love, where every heart beats,
In the garden of friendship, each life is complete.
Through seasons of change, let our spirits stay,
Boundless connections, guiding our way.

Threads of Renewal

In the fabric of time, threads intertwine,
Weaving our stories, yours and mine.
With colors of courage, hues of intent,
A tapestry rich, our journeys are lent.

Each dawn brings a promise, a canvas anew,
In the folds of our lives, bright patterns accrue.
Shedding old skins, embracing the light,
In the warmth of the sun, our spirits take flight.

As seasons awaken, with whispers of change,
We blossom like flowers, in spaces so strange.
Roots reaching deep, yet branches extend,
In the dance of renewal, our souls shall blend.

Moments of silence, reflections we find,
In the echoes of stillness, we refresh the mind.
With gratitude flowing, we cherish each day,
In the threads of our lives, together we sway.

So let us embrace, this journey divine,
With the threads of renewal, our spirits align.
In the fabric of love, forever we'll stay,
Woven together, come what may.

Embracing New Echoes

In the silence of night, echoes arise,
Whispers of change, under starlit skies.
With hearts wide open, we listen in tune,
To the calls of our dreams, like the softly sung moon.

Beyond the horizon, new paths await,
With each step we take, we welcome fate.
In the dance of the breeze, our souls ignite,
Embracing the echoes, of morning's first light.

Moments of joy, like notes that resound,
In the symphony of life, where love is profound.
Through valleys of whispers, through mountains of cheer,

We find our own rhythm, as we persevere.

With courage as guide, we journey unknown,
In the heart of the matter, together we've grown.
As echoes unfold, revealing the true,
We'll dance through the shadows, embracing the new.

So let us weave magic, in every refrain,
Through the echoes of time, our spirits remain.
With arms wide and hearts full, we shall not retreat,
Embracing new echoes, life feels complete.

The Embrace of Evolution

In the cradle of time, we start to grow,
Each step we take, the world starts to glow.
Nature whispers softly, guiding our way,
We learn to adapt, come what may.

With every sunrise, new paths unfold,
Stories of life in colors bold.
From humble beginnings, we rise and weave,
A tapestry of dreams we believe.

In shadows of doubt, we find our light,
Chasing the stars, we reach for the height.
In laughter and tears, we find our song,
In the dance of existence, we all belong.

With the heart of the earth, we beat in time,
In unison with nature, our spirits climb.
Embracing the changes, we find our place,
In the hands of evolution, we find grace.

Recasting Our Affection

In the quiet of evening, hearts unfold,
A journey of love, we dare to hold.
With whispers of kindness, we mend the threads,
Recasting affection, where two souls tread.

Each glance a promise, a silent vow,
In the bloom of trust, we learn to allow.
Through storms and sun, our spirits combine,
In the art of connection, our hearts intertwine.

The stories we share, a delicate weave,
In laughter and sorrow, we choose to believe.
With every heartbeat, we reshape our fate,
In the warmth of our bond, we celebrate.

As seasons change, so too do we grow,
Recasting our love in the softest glow.
From the ashes of doubt, new flames arise,
In the beauty of us, the world is our prize.

Blossoms in the Wind

Petals of hope dance in the breeze,
Whispering secrets among the trees.
In fragrant air, our dreams take flight,
Blossoms in the wind, a pure delight.

Each flower a story, each color a song,
In the garden of life, we all belong.
With the rustle of leaves, our hearts awaken,
Embracing the moments, unshaken, unbroken.

In the play of light, shadows intertwine,
Nature holds us close, in a love divine.
Through the rush of time, we stand hand in hand,
Rooted in trust, like trees we stand.

As seasons shift, our colors may fade,
Yet in every petal, our love is displayed.
With each gentle gust, we find our truth,
In the blossoms of youth, we cherish our roots.

Expanding Horizons

On the edge of dreams, we dare to stare,
With every horizon, new visions flare.
In the vastness of skies, our spirits soar,
Expanding horizons, forever explore.

With wings made of courage, we take to flight,
Charting new paths, guided by light.
The call of adventure beckons us near,
In the embrace of wonder, we conquer our fear.

Together we wander through forests of change,
In the beauty of growth, we rearrange.
With open hearts, we seek the unknown,
In the dance of discovery, we have grown.

As the world spins on, we cherish the ride,
In every sunrise, our hopes coincide.
Expanding horizons, hand in hand,
In the journey of life, together we stand.

Transformative Journeys

Beneath the stars, we start our quest,
Each step a whisper, time's own test.
Paths unknown, yet hearts ignite,
In shadows deep, we seek the light.

Mountains rise and rivers bend,
In every turn, we're forced to mend.
Voices call from far and wide,
With courage bold, we take the ride.

Moments fleeting, memories cling,
From every loss, new hope will spring.
Hands held tightly, fears we face,
In every heartbeat, we find grace.

With every dawn, a chance to grow,
In winds of change, we learn to flow.
Through valleys deep, we chase our dream,
Together strong, we're a mighty team.

When journeys end, new paths arise,
In every goodbye, a sweet surprise.
With visions clear, we carry on,
For in our hearts, the past is drawn.

Hearts in Flux

Rivers twist with tales untold,
Hearts evolve, they bend, unfold.
With every tear, a lesson learned,
In love's embrace, the passions burned.

Tender whispers in moonlit nights,
Shared secrets, endless delights.
Moments fleeting, yet they last,
In the present, we find the past.

Fleeting shadows, dreams take flight,
In silence deep, we find the light.
Through every storm, we stand in line,
In tangled emotions, our hearts align.

Through seasons change, feelings grow,
In every pulse, the truth we know.
With open hearts, we navigate,
For in this flux, we choose our fate.

With every pulse, a rhythm beats,
In vulnerability, love completes.
Two souls dancing, futures blend,
In this chaos, we find our end.

The Symphony of Us

In the quiet, a note we find,
A melody sweet, forever intertwined.
Each heartbeat plays a cherished tune,
Underneath the watchful moon.

In the echoes of laughter bright,
We compose with warmth and light.
Harmonies unique, voices blend,
Every chorus, our hearts transcend.

Rhythms pulse through open hearts,
As the dance of love imparts.
With every whisper, joy expands,
In unity, we take our stands.

Notes of sorrow, bittersweet,
In the symphony, we find our feet.
Through crescendos, we learn to rise,
In every challenge, wisdom lies.

Together, we write our song anew,
With every trial, we push on through.
A timeless ballad, forever flows,
In the symphony of us, love grows.

Tides of Transition

Waves of change, they crash and swell,
With every tide, a truth to tell.
In ebb and flow, we find our way,
Guiding stars, light our stay.

Moments shifting like grains of sand,
In time's embrace, we learn to stand.
With every whisper, winds of fate,
We rise anew, we contemplate.

Seas of doubt may pull us low,
In every swell, we learn to grow.
The journey wide, horizons vast,
In every heartbeat, echoes past.

In quiet depths, reflections shine,
Through storms and trials, we redefine.
With open hearts, the tide we'll face,
For transformation holds its grace.

As dawn breaks soft on distant shores,
We chase the dreams that time restores.
In every wave, a chance to soar,
Through tides of change, we seek for more.

Branching Out

In the soft glow of dawn's light,
Branches reach out, a beautiful sight.
Leaves unfurl with whispers sweet,
Nature's dance, a rhythmic beat.

Beneath the skies, we take flight,
Exploring dreams that feel so right.
With every step, we learn and grow,
Paths unknown begin to flow.

Roots run deep, in soil we trust,
Nurtured hopes turn into dust.
Yet from the earth, new life will sprout,
Embracing change, we're branching out.

In every shadow, there's a chance,
For light to break, for hearts to dance.
So take my hand, let's forge a way,
Together, we'll greet each day.

Beneath the stars, our stories weave,
In every laugh, in every leave.
With open arms, we face the night,
In this journey, feel the light.

Echoes of Discovery

Through the mist of time we roam,
Every whisper holds a home.
Ancient paths invite our gaze,
In every corner, secrets blaze.

With curious hearts, we tread the ground,
In silence, echoes softly sound.
Hidden truths arise and play,
Like shadows that dance at the end of day.

Each new discovery, a spark ignites,
In endless quests, we chase the lights.
Through valleys deep and mountains high,
We learn to soar, we learn to fly.

Wisdom shared like raindrops fall,
Filling cups, we share it all.
In every moment, laughter found,
Life's vast canvas, so profound.

Together we weave our dreams anew,
In every heartbeat, a world so true.
Under the vast expanse, we sing,
The echoes of discovery take wing.

Heartbeats in Harmony

In the hush of twilight's embrace,
Heartbeats join in a sacred space.
Rhythms echo, a gentle tune,
In every glance, beneath the moon.

Whispers of love, soft and clear,
Each moment shared, forever dear.
Two souls weaving, a fabric fine,
In trust's embrace, our hearts align.

Through storms and calm, we sail the sea,
Finding solace, you and me.
Like waves that crash and kiss the shore,
Together we rise, forevermore.

Notes of laughter fill the air,
A symphony beyond compare.
With every heartbeat, we create,
A melody that will not wait.

In harmony, our spirits soar,
With every step, we dance and explore.
In love's embrace, we find our way,
Two heartbeats echo, come what may.

New Seasons of Trust

As winter fades, the flowers bloom,
In every heart, there’s room.
Spring brings promise, fresh and bright,
New seasons call, inviting light.

With every dawn, trust starts to grow,
Like rivers flowing, pure and slow.
Hand in hand, we turn the page,
With every word, we build a stage.

In the warmth of summer's glow,
Our bond strengthens, love will show.
Through trials faced, we learn to stay,
Sowing seeds along the way.

As leaves turn gold and fall from trees,
We embrace change with gentle ease.
In autumn's grace, we find our path,
Creating joy beyond mere math.

Trust like roots, deep in the earth,
Nurtured stories, holding worth.
Through every season, side by side,
New chapters written, love our guide.

Whispers of New Beginnings

In dawn's light softly gleams,
Hope unfurls like summer dreams.
Each moment whispers, take your chance,
With open hearts, we start to dance.

The past drifts like a fading cloud,
New choices rise and feel so proud.
Tender hopes take flight anew,
In skies painted with shades of blue.

A breath of promise fills the air,
In each heartbeat, blessings share.
The world awaits our steps ahead,
With courage sewn, we'll weave our thread.

Echoes of laughter spark the day,
In unity, we find our way.
Let go the chains that held us tight,
Embrace the dawn, the shining light.

Together we will forge a path,
With joy and love, we'll cherish math.
The future whispers, bold and bright,
In every shadow, find the light.

Hearts Unbound

In twilight's glow, we find our truth,
Two souls entwined, embraced in youth.
No walls can cage what love has sown,
With every heartbeat, bonds have grown.

Through storms and trials, side by side,
We journey forth, our hearts our guide.
Each secret shared, a thread so fine,
In every moment, your hand in mine.

In laughter's song, we dance as one,
The weight of worries swiftly shun.
With whispered dreams, we'll paint the night,
In starlit skies, our spirits flight.

The paths we walk, both wild and true,
With courage found, there's much to do.
In every glance, a thousand words,
Our love, a song, forever heard.

Together we'll write our own refrain,
In joy and sorrow, sunshine, rain.
With hearts unbound, we claim our course,
In unity, we find our source.

Refreshing the Bond

Amongst the trees, the whispers sway,
Friendships bloom in splendid array.
With laughter shared, and stories spun,
We weave the threads, our hearts as one.

In seasons changing, roots run deep,
Through life's vast ocean, memories keep.
A glance, a touch, a knowing smile,
Each moment treasured, worth the while.

With open hearts, we dance in sync,
In gentle words, our spirits link.
Through every trial, stand side by side,
In unity, we take this ride.

An echo calls to times once missed,
With every hug, a bond we twist.
In silent joys, we find our grace,
In every heartbeat, love's embrace.

So here's to us, the ties we weave,
With every season, we believe.
Refreshing bonds, strong and true,
In every chapter, me and you.

New Narratives

In pages blank, the stories wait,
With pen in hand, we write our fate.
Each word a spark, igniting dreams,
In whispered hopes, the future gleams.

With every line, we build anew,
The tales of us, unfolding true.
A dance of fate, in ink reside,
Through every chapter, hearts collide.

In vibrant ink, our colors blend,
The path unwritten, around bend.
With courage penned, we face romance,
Together forging every chance.

In twilight hours, our voices rise,
Each laugh, each tear, a sweet reprise.
In timeless echoes, we persist,
In every moment, love can't resist.

So take my hand, let's share this ride,
In every word, our stories guide.
New narratives await, let's explore,
In every heartbeat, we'll soar.

Beyond the Familiar

In shadows cast by old regrets,
We step towards the bright unknown.
Each moment whispers, softly beckons,
To leave behind the past we've sown.

With courage wrapped in silken dreams,
We venture forth, hearts intertwined.
Embracing change, as daylight streams,
Into the depths of soul and mind.

The path ahead can twist and turn,
Yet hope ignites the darkest night.
In every step, a spark will burn,
Guiding us toward the morning light.

Not bound by fears, but lifted high,
We chase the rhythms of the skies.
Beyond the familiar, we will fly,
On wings of chance, our spirits rise.

So here we stand, together bold,
With dreams anew, we boldly strive.
Beyond the familiar, we behold,
The endless wonders that arrive.

Blossoms from Ashes

When all seems lost and dark the day,
From ashes springs a vibrant bloom.
In fields once barren, hope finds way,
Transforming grief into sweet perfume.

Each petal soft, a tale to tell,
Of struggles faced and lessons learned.
Through stormy nights, we rise and swell,
With fiery will, our spirits burned.

Though shadows whisper doubts and fears,
Resilience roots beneath the stone.
A dance of joy amidst the tears,
We find the strength to stand alone.

In every heart that dares to fight,
Are seeds of purpose waiting true.
With every breath, we claim our right,
To blossom bold, as morning dew.

So here’s to life, in every phase,
From ashes, beauty finds its place.
In tangled paths, we weave our ways,
Creating treasures we embrace.

The Dance of Rebirth

With every dawn, a chance unfolds,
A rhythm pulsing, fresh and bright.
In nature's hands, the tale retold,
Of life renewed in soft twilight.

As whispers flow on gentle tides,
Awakening the sleeping ground,
In every heart, a moment guides,
The dance of spirit, love unbound.

Through trials faced and lessons learned,
We find our way, our voices swell.
In every step, a fire burned,
Illuminates the paths we dwell.

Together we sway in unity,
Embracing every rise and fall.
In harmony, we find the key,
To life's grand dance, we heed the call.

So let us weave this tapestry,
With colors bold, both bright and rare.
Through joy and pain, in ecstasy,
We celebrate the dance we share.

Bridges We Build

Across the chasm, hearts extend,
With open arms and trust to share.
In every bond, a tale we send,
Creating hope from silent prayer.

Through storms that rage and winds that howl,
A bridge of strength forms wise and true.
With each connection, we avow,
In unity, we will break through.

Though differences may stand between,
Compassion's hand can reach the side.
With tender words, we form the scene,
Where understanding serves as guide.

From brick to stone, in laughter's glow,
We pave a way with love as guide.
In every step, together go,
On bridges wide, with hearts open wide.

So let us build, with every breath,
A world where kindness reigns in time.
Through bridges strong, we conquer death,
In love's embrace, our spirits climb.

From Ashes to Affection

In the shadows, a spark resides,
Memories fade, but love abides.
From the ruins, we rise and glow,
Healing hearts, a gentle flow.

Through the pain, we learn to trust,
Building dreams from fallen dust.
With each step, a bond we weave,
In the darkest nights, we believe.

Hands entwined, we face the storm,
From grief's ashes, a new form.
In the warmth of a shared embrace,
We find strength in time and space.

Whispers linger, soft and sweet,
In our journey, love complete.
Together, we'll rewrite the tale,
From the embers, we'll set sail.

Every scar tells a story bright,
Through the chaos, we found light.
In the fire, affection blooms,
A testament that love consumes.

Cultivating Deeper Roots

In the garden where silence speaks,
Nurturing dreams beneath the peaks.
Seeds of hope in the fertile ground,
In patience, our love is found.

With tender hands, we plant our care,
In every moment, a silent prayer.
We water trust with gentle grace,
Through storms, we hold our sacred space.

Roots entwined, a steadfast bond,
In the soil, we feel life's fond.
With every drop, we tend our hearts,
In blooming love, a brand new start.

Cultivating whispers of the night,
In twilight's glow, we find our light.
Each blossom sings a song of hope,
Together, we learn, together, we cope.

Through seasons change, we stand so tall,
In unity, we conquer all.
Deeper roots, a life we share,
In nature's arms, we breathe the air.

Hand in hand, we walk this path,
Harvest love, a sweet aftermath.
In the garden, we find our truth,
Cultivating always our sweet youth.

The Mosaic of Us

Fragments scattered on the floor,
Each piece tells a tale of more.
In colors bright, and shadows deep,
Through the cracks, our memories seep.

With patience, we assemble the frame,
In every corner, we shape the same.
Tiles of laughter, moments shared,
In every chip, a heart laid bare.

Together, we craft a grand design,
In every heartbeat, a thread divine.
A vibrant picture, a life combined,
In the silence, our souls aligned.

The light reflects on every hue,
In every step, a love renewed.
With gentle hands, we place each stone,
In the mosaic, we are never alone.

Through storms that try to break apart,
We stitch the pieces, heart to heart.
An endless journey, a work of art,
In the mosaic, we play our part.

Every crack holds a story told,
In the warmth, we find our gold.
The beauty lies in the cracks of trust,
In the mosaic of us, we must.

Unexpected Blooms

In the dust, a petal sighs,
Amidst the chaos, beauty lies.
From concrete cracks, a flower breaks,
With vibrant hues, the heart awakes.

With gentle winds, the seeds are sown,
In barren lands, we find our own.
Through struggles, fragile dreams ignite,
Unexpected blooms, a pure delight.

Beneath the weight of endless skies,
In shadowed corners, hope will rise.
With every drop of falling rain,
In gentle ways, we ease the pain.

Delicate petals in morning's light,
In every struggle, joy takes flight.
Together we cultivate our grace,
In the garden, we find our place.

As seasons change, new blossoms greet,
In every moment, love's heartbeat.
Through trials faced, we learn to bloom,
Unexpected beauty, dispelling gloom.

In the quiet, we find our peace,
With every bloom, the heart's release.
In life's embrace, we rise and fall,
Unexpected blooms, we cherish all.

Fresh Perspectives

A dawn breaks with hues anew,
Shadows dance, revealing view.
Thoughts unbound, we're set to soar,
Looking closer, seeking more.

Eyes wide open, truths unfold,
Stories whispered, tales retold.
Beneath the surface, clarity,
In every moment, we are free.

Roots begin to twist and grow,
Nature's pulse begins to show.
With every breath, all things align,
In the stillness, patterns shine.

A canvas stretched, colors blend,
Different angles, hearts extend.
In our hands, creation sings,
Each unique, all have wings.

What was lost can now be found,
Wisdom echoes all around.
With patience, we redefine,
In the now, our stars align.

Evolving Hearts

In silence, hearts begin to bloom,
A gentle touch dispels the gloom.
With every heartbeat, courage grows,
In compassion, love overflows.

Laughter shared, a fleeting glance,
With every risk, we find romance.
Wounds will heal, and scars will fade,
In the sun, our fears will wade.

Paths may twist, but we're not lost,
Finding strength in every cost.
Through warm embrace, we're intertwined,
In the journey, peace we find.

Every tear tells its own tale,
Though we stumble, we will sail.
With open arms, we face the night,
For in darkness, there’s still light.

Voices blend, a sweet refrain,
In joy and sorrow, love remains.
Every heartbeat, a brand new start,
Together now, evolving heart.

Shifting Dynamics

In a dance of give and take,
The world turns, and paths will shake.
Fragile balance, ever strange,
With moments spent, we rearrange.

Ideas clash, but minds expand,
Seeds of change are sown by hand.
In conversations, sparks ignite,
Navigating through the night.

What was certain now feels strange,
In the flow, we find our range.
With every shift, we understand,
In the chaos, we take a stand.

Ebb and flow, like waves that break,
In the tides, new paths we make.
Lessons learned, we forge ahead,
In the shifting, no more dread.

With open hearts, we rearrange,
Building bridges from the change.
Stronger together, we will strive,
In every challenge, we arrive.

Harmonies Rediscovered

In echoes past, a melody,
Resonating deep in me.
Notes entwined, a symphony,
Together crafting harmony.

In quiet moments, souls collide,
Amidst the noise, we're not divide.
With hands outstretched, we reach for light,
In unity, we find our might.

Voices blend, rich and true,
Every tone creates anew.
From whispered dreams to shouts of joy,
In every heart, we find a buoy.

Dancing rhythms, swift and free,
In the flow, we’re meant to be.
As time unfolds, the music swells,
In each heartbeat, magic dwells.

Casting aside doubts that bind,
A brighter path we seek to find.
In every story, every part,
Together we'll create art.

Milton Keynes UK
Ingram Content Group UK Ltd.
UKHW021824311024
450535UK00010B/197

9 789916 890080